Dr. Bill Saye (signature)

"Mister, Can You Help Me?"

The story of a street kid named
GOPEE

—&—

Bill Saye

Published by

LifeBridge
B o o k s
P.O. BOX 49428
CHARLOTTE, NC 28277

Printed in the United States of America.

Dedication

*T his book is dedicated first, to
my friend Robert, "Gopee," and second,
to all my fellow workers who pray and go
into the world preaching the Gospel
of our Lord Jesus Christ.
God bless you all!*

Acknowledgments

I want to thank my children, most of all, for standing by me after everything I've put them through. Tammy, Brenda, Bill, Jr., and Eddie – Thanks! I love you.

My church and my Pastor Den Weniger for the encouragement they have been to me.

All my friends who work with me in ministry, both on the streets and in prisons.

And especially my new wife who God graciously gave me in 1988. Vicki, I love you, darling.

And to those who help our ministry with your prayers and financial support. Thank you for being a part of all we do as we present Christ to a hurting world.

Contents

1

The Face in the Window

I t was a day like any other, at least for the last few years. Like any other morning, I was up at 5 A.M. The way the sun was shining, it really was a beautiful day. As I dressed, I thought of my schedule – full as usual. On my way into the city, I decided to stop at a restaurant and eat breakfast.

Finding a place near the window, I thought about how different it was a few years ago. I would have never sat by the window. It was too easy to be seen and recognized; too easy a target. I was thankful I could enjoy the daylight once again without that worry.

My "Kingdom"

A runaway at age 12, a gang member at 13 and a gang leader at 14, I had been arrested numerous times, shot twice, had two homes burned, a number of death threats made on my life, my wife murdered, my son kidnaped, and I thought I was some kind of god.

Materially, I had everything the world had to offer. I ran a five-state prostitution ring and later became head of the largest drug organization of its type in the USA. I became a multimillionaire and thought I had it all.

I was arrested for first-degree murder...and was told I would die in the electric chair.

I was known as the "Drug King" with an empire, but in 1980, my "Kingdom" came to an end when I was arrested for first-degree murder. I lost everything and was told I would die in the electric chair.

But because of 40 years of faithful prayer by my parents, God spared me.

I've Been There!

On September 24th, 1982, as the result of a major chain of events in my efforts to be freed by man-made ways and failing, God was able to intervene. He saved my soul and changed my life forever! Although I was not set free from prison, I was liberated from the bondage of sin.

I am now a full time evangelist, ministering in

churches, schools, prisons, and in the streets of our cities. I believe because of my past life, I have something to offer hurting people of all walks of life through our Lord Jesus Christ.

What Was He Looking At?

On this particular morning my mind was racing through all the things I needed to get done. The last thing I expected was to look up and see a reflection of myself staring back at me through the window. My breakfast came and I bowed my head in thanks. As I lifted my head, the busy schedule scrolled by in my imagination as I unthinkingly salted and peppered my eggs. Then my eyes met the haunting eyes of a young boy in my window. He was not looking at me, but at my breakfast. Hungry, dressed in worn and dirty clothes, his face was a little dusty as he stared intently at my food.

"I Was Hungry"

We don't realize there are so many hungry people in America, but there are, right before us. It was as if the Lord was reminding me of the scripture in the New Testament: *"For I was hungry and you gave me something to eat, I was thirsty and you gave me something to drink, I was a stranger and you invited me in. I needed clothes and you clothed me, I was sick and you looked after me, I was in prison and you came to visit me"* (Matthew 25:35-36 NIV).

I was too busy to hear the Lord just then as this young boy captured my attention.

Suddenly he realized I was looking at him. He dropped his head, his long matted hair swung as he turned, and started to walk away. It was only then that I could see he wasn't wearing any shoes. No shoes . . . bare feet . . . I started to remember when I had no shoes . . .

"Look at Bill's Feet!"

My parents were poor, and shoes were a luxury we couldn't afford. I remembered walking over the cold, wet ground to the old schoolhouse, and sitting as close as I could to a pot-belly stove heater without drawing too much attention to myself. Season after season, I walked into school barefoot. Then in the fourth grade class, my teacher called me to the front of the room.

"Bill, would you please come up here and stand by me?" Maybe she was trying to help, or perhaps she was trying to stop the other children's teasing by having them understand my situation, but all her efforts backfired.

"Now class, I want you to look at Bill's feet . . ."

– whatever she said after that are forgotten words. All I recall was everyone laughing at me – at my feet. I ran out of the class, and did not return. I was mortified. My greatest fear was set, and I promised myself I would never be without shoes ever again. No matter what it took to get the money needed, I vowed I wouldn't be that poor again. I never was, but this vow almost cost me my life.

What was God Saying?

As my memories faded into "eggs-going-cold" reality, I hurriedly ate my breakfast, left the tip, paid the bill, and pulled my car into the highway. I thought no more of this young kid who sparked my own memories of living "on the streets," and ignored the small voice inside me.

My greatest fear was set, and I promised myself I would never be without shoes ever again.

I was 12 years old when I left home for the streets and gangs. More memories started to swirl, but the "importance" of my first meeting drove through these thoughts as I stepped on the gas pedal. A few blocks later, tempting tickets, fines, and caution lights, the scripture returned to my mind.

"I was hungry, and you fed me not... I was naked, and you clothed me not . . . I was in prison, and you visited me not . . . I was sick, and you comforted me not . . ."

"I was hungry, and you fed me not...I was naked and you clothed me not...I was in prison and you visited me not..."

Then followed a more personal paraphrase: "I was barefoot, and you gave me no shoes."

"I Never Knew You"

Annoyed with the Lord's interruption, I finally blurted out, "God, what are you trying to say to me?"

He didn't take long to reply, "This is where a lot of people are . . . Do you remember the scripture? *Thus, by their fruit you will recognize them. Not everyone who says to me, 'Lord, Lord,' will enter the kingdom of heaven. But only he who does the will of my Father who is in heaven. Many will say to me on that day 'Lord, Lord, did we not prophesy in your name, and in your name drive out demons and perform many miracles?' Then I will tell them plainly, 'I never knew you. Away from me, you evildoers!"* (Matthew 7:20-23 (NIV).

My heart was pricked . . . the young boy in the window came into my mind blending with the thoughts of my own childhood and what I thought was depravity. The memory of my 9:30 A.M. appointment faded, being replaced with the impressions the Lord was making on my heart and mind.

Could He Love Me?

The recollection of my school days was vivid. I could still almost taste the pain I felt in that elementary school as I ran down the hall saying to myself, "When I grow up I'll never be barefoot even if I have to kill someone for shoes."

I could still almost taste the pain I felt in that elementary school...

I couldn't understand how anyone could love me. I used to think, "If my parents truly cared they would buy me some shoes to wear to school."

At that age I didn't comprehend my dad was doing all he could, making only twelve dollars and fifty cents a week. I remembered how we would stand in the classroom and recite the Lord's Prayer and sing "Jesus loves me, this I know for the Bible tells me so." While at the same time, the kids would be laughing at my feet.

I didn't think anyone even liked me. Certainly not Jesus. How could He possibly love a barefoot boy in the fourth grade who hated his classmates and harbored such hurt in his heart the way I did?

"Let the Children Come"

Just then, as Jesus so often does, I was reminded of how He rebuked the disciples for keeping the children from Him. It must have been a stern look and a strong voice that said, *"Let the little children come to me, and do not hinder them, for the kingdom of heaven belongs to such as these"* (Matthew 19:14).

I was no more important than a grain of sand in a great big world, or so I thought.

Jesus wanted to hold them, to let those children know that somebody cared.

How lonely it was for me in the days of my street life. No one to talk to, and no one to turn to. I was no more important than a grain of sand in a great big world, or so I thought.

"Just One More Chance"

Again, the face of this boy woke me from my daydreaming. "Oh God," I said, realizing I was missing a life-changing opportunity, "Forgive me . . . please Lord, give me another opportunity . . . Just let me have one more chance!"

2

"The Name is Gopee"

realized I had passed the meeting place for my appointment, and made a u-turn, still thinking I could possibly make it. With the city traffic heavy with commuters, I decided to turn down a small street to save time. The street narrowed with abandoned cars and furniture of some dispossessed family which further constricted my passage, forcing me to slow down.

At the next corner, low and behold, there he was – the boy in my window. I was so happy I thought my heart would jump out of my shirt! Ten thousand thoughts raced through my mind. "Oh! Thank you, Lord," I thought, and then it hit me. What would I say to this young street-smart kid? I asked God to give me wisdom to say or do something to get his attention.

He was leaning into the open window of a luxury car, and talking to a man. I was so elated to be offered my second chance with the boy that I braked the car sharply. I probably looked like an undercover cop, for the man panicked and sped off. The young boy turned and shouted, "Mister, you don't know what you did!"

Anger filled the mouth of this street-tough kid and again my heart melted for him.

"I was trying to get some money for breakfast!" he said.

"I was trying to get some money for breakfast!" he said. His arms lifted and fell in frustration.

Turning back, he watched his last hope seemingly disappear with the car and its settling dust cloud.

Selling Their Bodies

This is the place where young boys sell themselves for a meal. In this area of town you can find young girls and boys hanging out on the street corners at almost any time of the day or night, offering their bodies for money to buy a meal or drugs. Some are there because their gang forces them to do it – to raise money to support the gang.

"How About Some Breakfast?"

I must have looked like a guy in a big hurry to

make a bust or make a score. I jumped out of my car and shouted, "Son, what's your name?" with my hand reaching into my pocket.

The boy looked at me and the "hustle-look" appeared in his eyes. "The name is Gopee."

Later I found out his name was Robert . . . "Gopee" was his street-name, and he was certainly "on-the-streets."

"You got something for me, mister?" he asked as his eyes looked up to mine and then back to my hand.

"How about some breakfast, Gopee?" I suggested.

"Eggs scrambled and . . . I want some country ham!" Gopee was adamant, and I agreed with his order.

The little restaurant was full of on-lookers, but it didn't matter, Gopee was telling me his short life's story while anxiously awaiting his food. The customers were glancing at me like I was a dirty old man. But I really didn't care what they thought. I was so pleased to have the chance to hear this boy's story.

3

An Abandoned Kid

I t was an unexpected story at first. He told me how his mother and father were so happy together when Gopee was a small boy. Everything, it seemed, was going well for them.

A contented child, Gopee was from a moderate income family who bought him a bike at age four. At six Gopee even had a go-kart. They lived in a nice home in the suburbs and went camping together whenever they could.

Gopee told me how his Dad taught him to hit a ball, and how they played football out on the front lawn. "We went to church a couple of times," he said, "usually around Easter and Christmas. All in all, that was the best times, man!"

An "Added Expense"

Gopee stared past me towards some distant scenes

only he could see in the restaurant window. Then his face changed from the smiles of pleasant memories into one large sad frown, bitter with remorse.

He was remembering the emptiness from the day his father "just up and left," as Gopee put it. He ran away and never came back. His mother tried hard to save the family's house, getting different waitressing jobs, but could never make ends meet.

Because of the stress, she began to drink. At age ten, Gopee realized his now alcoholic mother was venting her bitter frustrations on him. She would beat him, make him go to his room without food, and one time he was forced to stay in a closet a whole day. To make matters worse, his mom turned to drugs, and when money ran out, she became a prostitute to keep her habit going.

Finally, it became evident that Gopee was an "added expense" to her. He was forced to leave. At first he thought his mother was kidding. Surely it was just the drugs talking. This was his mother – how could she possibly want her child to leave their home? But her boyfriend came on the scene and hit Gopee, telling him to grab his clothes and get his butt out of there.

Kicked Out

With tears in his eyes, Gopee, began reliving the

pain all over again. I wanted to put my arms around him and tell him I understood and that I loved him. But, knowing the street code, I held back as he continued.

His mother easily agreed with her boyfriend and Gopee was kicked out.

The Game – The Pain!

This was an account I had heard many times before. Dealing with street kids over the years, I have listened to many such horror stories. I know some kids make up these tales just to win sympathy, but not Gopee. You could see the deep hurt in his eyes.

Without question, the eyes are the windows of one's soul. I know this from my own life on the streets. There is a saying among street people, "If you've never played the game, don't try to tell me about the pain."

"If you've never played the game, don't try to tell me about the pain."

I could feel Gopee's pain – the loneliness, the emptiness that no one even knows you're alive. Gopee had no family to turn to, no relatives, so he went into the streets. Lonely, cold and hungry most of the time, he learned to beg for food. He slept in a myriad of different places.

One night, curled up under some steps, he woke to a violent rainstorm. He was wet and shivering with cold; no place to go. So he remained huddled under the stairs waiting for the end of the rain, or himself, whichever would come first.

Finally the rain subsided, and the process of finding food for the day began once again.

4

Dude, the Dealer

The local hamburger joint was the best place for Gopee to find food because they tossed out the old hamburgers. At night, he could squeeze himself into the trash bin area and eat as much as his stomach could hold. Then the fast-food chain bought a large garbage compactor and Gopee lost his only food source overnight. Not only was food scarce, but life was getting harder.

One day, while trying to hustle some money from a passer-by, Gopee saw a man coming toward him. He thought, "Here comes somebody big." So he began to talk to the man and the fellow answered in a friendly way.

"Dude" was impressive. The leader of a local street gang who didn't fit the stereotype of the typical gang leader. He was a masculine, 25 year-old with a mustache, which impressed Gopee the most. Well dressed with gold chains and a large gold ring, Dude's name fit his image. So when this man talked to Gopee, the young lad stopped and listened.

"My name's Robert," Gopee confided in Dude.

"Well, you can call me 'Dude'. . . Okay, bro'?"

Dude smiled, holding his hand out to be "slapped five" and Gopee smiled back, completing the hand ritual. Gopee began to feel as if he belonged. As for Dude, that was exactly the response he wanted from Gopee.

The "American Way"

In America, drug-dealers go to jail, but only when they get caught dealing. Minors caught with drugs, even when they are dealing drugs, rarely go to prison. So for the drug-dealers, young street kids were the perfect "delivery system."

The way the dealers and gang leaders work much of the time is this: they find a young person who receives little or no attention at home, usually because both parents work either by choice or necessity. The child is left alone during the week and on weekends the parents are too busy to spend quality time with their kids, leaving the door wide open for gangs and drug pushers to befriend them.

And so it begins, the process of indoctrination into the world of darkness.

"It's the 'American Way'!" Dude would say to his suppliers. This is what he had in mind for Gopee, but sadly, the young man had no idea what Dude was up to, or what lay ahead for him.

A Father Figure

Dude began to give Gopee what he needed. First, Dude paid for breakfast, and found him a place to sleep. Then Gopee was given some new clothes, and finally a brand new pair of shoes. Gopee was happier than he'd ever been – almost as happy as when he used to play with his father.

For Gopee, the pleasant memories of his dad began to blur into the image of Dude. He was confused, but the feeling of being warm and accepted overcame any uneasiness. In fact, Gopee was fast becoming a devoted follower of his new

Gopee was fast becoming a devoted follower of his new benefactor.

benefactor, Dude, and would probably do anything for him.

"Within reason!" Gopee would say to himself, but less and less was becoming unreasonable.

"All you got to do is take a couple of these small packages to where they need to go . . . That's it, Gopee . . . No need to know nothing else, see?"

Dude's lieutenant held out the brown-wrapped

drugs. Gopee knew it wouldn't always be drugs; sometimes it would contain money. Every now and then it would be a decoy package made to look real to frustrate the cops when they "busted" you. It was almost a game. Almost . . . except for the "druggies" who Gopee met in the alleys with glazed, half-closed eyes as they huddled over the last "shoot-up," generally alone, always gaunt and skeletal as the drugs took their deadly effect.

These real pictures stripped "the game" of its fun.

5

The Hook

As we mentioned, Gopee's real name was Robert, but his association with Dude's gang got him his "street" name.

For Robert, growing up on the street was nutritionally devastating. He acquired a kidney infection which caused him to urinate frequently. To others, his constant refrain of, "I've got to go pee," earned him his title, "Gopee" and it stuck!

As ignoble as his nickname was, money in the drug business made up for a lot. Gopee finally had cash to spend. He could eat when he pleased, buy clothes and shoes when he wanted, go to the movies or a stage play. He even got to ride in a Corvette Stingray.

Dude liked Gopee, and gave him extra jobs which meant even more money. Everything was going well! Deliveries were good, money was there, and Gopee was happy.

Then Dude left town without telling Gopee. What

he didn't know was that Dude was picking up a large drug shipment and decided to stay overnight.

Alone again, Gopee's fears overtook his mind. His sense of losing his "friend" led to imagining himself abandoned on the streets once more. He desired those "good feelings" again, but how?

Happy Faces?

What came to his mind could only have been placed there by Satan himself. Distorted thoughts of continued rejection caused Gopee to retreat to his familiar memories of a happier childhood. Only this time, the sense of loss overwhelmed him like never before. Everyone was leaving . . . he was alone . . . perhaps forever this time!

Slowly a picture began to form. It was one of smiling faces, of street people like himself, of individuals he knew. The faces took shape. They were smiling, joking with one another, just the way Gopee wanted to be, only these were the faces of the customers he sold the drugs to! They were so elated – happy he had brought them their drugs!

Drugs! Was that the answer? Gopee didn't want the weight of sadness anymore. He just wanted to be happy, as he thought these people were.

"Look at their faces!" a voice whispered. Gopee stared into the mirror of a darkened room. He couldn't distinguish the voice from his own thinking.

"You'd be smiling too, if you took those drugs!"

"Drugs? Me?" Gopee blurted.

"Not a lot, just enough to get carefree!" the voice said reassuringly.

"Oh . . . not too much to get hooked or nuthin'."

"No . . . You won't get hooked!" the voice promised. There was almost a distant chuckle, but Gopee dismissed it. He was hell-bent to find the happiness that eluded him – just like those who took their drugs. Gopee was convinced he would go from his depression to utter euphoria!

The Spiders!

It was their misguided solution to the bad things in this world, and it would be his too, not realizing he would be like the 14 year old girl in another city.

*"The spiders,
the spiders.
They're in
my eyes!"*

Desperately wanting to be accepted, she took her first taste of the so called "good life" when a 19 year old boy offered her a joint of pot laced with angel dust. In a few minutes she began to scream, "The spiders, the spiders. They're in my eyes!"

With her fingers she plucked out her own eye

balls. This girl overcame the drugs, but will spend the rest of her life in total darkness.

"That's My Family!"

No one wants to be alone. The gangs know this and lead kids to think if they will join up with them, they will never be lonely again – they will be accepted, have a place to live, and friends who will always be there.

But as I have traveled the nation going into prisons and Youth Detention Centers, I always ask, "How many of you belong to a gang?" Many hands are raised. Then I question, "Did your gang tell you they would love you and be your family – and if anyone got in your face they would throw them out?"

They nod their heads and say, "Yeah, man, that's my family!" Then I ask, "How many of your gang members have accepted a collect phone call from you since you've been in here?" The smile always disappears from their faces.

I've not had one say their gang had accepted such a call. Nor have I seen any of these young kids being supported by their gang while incarcerated. Most of them had no idea what they were getting into when they entered this world of darkness.

You see, it is not the second, third, tenth or even the fiftieth time you do drugs that gets you, it's always the first time. Without it, the door of depravity would forever remain closed.

Looking for Love

"How much time did your parents spend with you when you were at home?" is a question I also ask these young gang members in prison.

Most of them laughed, "My folks hardly knew I was alive, much less spent time with me."

Then I question, "How often did they tell you, 'I love you'?" The usual response is, "Huh, I can't remember the last time my folks said that to each other, let alone to me."

"My folks hardly knew I was alive, much less spent time with me."

On occasion, I have the opportunity to visit some of these inmates' families and I always ask the parents how much time they spent with their child before he or she got into trouble. Many times the mother defensively responds, "Well, I was here everyday when they came home from school." But when I push the issue, I learn the youngster was in his room on the computer while mom was watching her soaps! Being in the same house together is not the same as spending time with one another.

35

I ask them, "How often did you put your arms around your children and tell them, 'I love you'?" Many times the father would respond, "My son knows I love him. I don't have to say it. He knows. Look at all the things I've given him."

Material gifts are no substitute for the words, "I love you." It usually means you are trying to "buy them off" so you don't have to give of yourself. Instead, they need a bear hug and an "I love you" more than anything you can purchase.

Gopee was about to enter that world; the black hole drugs put your mind in as it takes possession of your life.

Remember, love is not for sale. That's why so many people are drawn into the world of darkness and drugs. They are lonely and desperate, looking for someone, anyone, to say three simple words, "I love you" – and mean it!

The Craving

Gopee was about to enter that world; the black hole drugs put your mind in as it takes possession of your life. He thought it would be the answer to his depression.

He took his first hit of crack cocaine, and from that moment, he was not just delivering drugs, he was using them. He went from making money to spending whatever he made on his own drug habit.

No longer was Gopee selling drugs for his food, clothing and shoes. He *had* to sell to support his insatiable craving for drugs.

He found out too late it wasn't the second or third "hit" that ensnares you, it is the first one that does you in. He was "hooked" the first time he tried it, like so many others.

Losing Control

With each passing day of his drug habit, his money diminished. Dude smiled every time Gopee paid for his drugs. Now, in need of a fix, Dude controlled every aspect of his life.

"Look at him go. . ." Dude would say as he laughed at Gopee, "We don't have to worry if he'll come back!"

"He's hooked real bad, man." The lieutenant looked back as Gopee toked the crack cocaine, and smiled, saying, "Took a double hit rocker that time."

"Good. . . real good!" Dude had much in mind for Gopee, and believe me, none of it was good.

I know full well how easy it is to gain control over people who are addicted. I've seen young girls who would never think of prostitution giving their bodies willingly for their drug habit. There was nothing that would stand in the way of getting the cocaine or heroin they needed. They would gladly do whatever we said.

6

"Don't Hit Me Again!"

Waves of shame still overwhelm me at times when I think about what I did. I need to remind myself constantly that the Blood of Jesus Christ covers my confessed sins; my guilt is washed away. Still, the grace and mercy I receive propels me to the streets to tell others like Gopee there is hope for them as well.

Let me offer some free advice. For those who haven't started down this tragic trail, don't! It always begins as a friendly gesture. Some older guy usually makes an offer and then they act like you are not mature enough, or man enough, to follow through. They know they can place peer pressure on you if you hesitate. They try hard to get the girls to do the drugs, knowing if they get hooked, they have a built-in source of revenue. Perverted older men will pay well for a young teenage girl. How well I know about that!

When I was in the prostitution business we would go to where the teens hung out and mix with them, finding out who was a leader and work through him to get info on the kids who were vulnerable, lonely and wanting to fit in. In a short time we would have those kids in our back pockets!

On Credit?

Parents have no idea how easy it is to lure their sons and daughters into gangs and drugs. The set-up man will usually give the kids their first drugs free, knowing that after they're hooked many of them can't get enough money from their parents to supply their habit. So the leader or supplier will simply say the magic word: "Credit."

"You'll let me have credit?" Gopee gasped in disbelief.

"You'll let me have credit?" Gopee gasped in disbelief.

"Sure, man! I trust you. I know you'll be good for it later." Dude smiled. He knew Gopee was getting in over his head. That's right where Dude wanted him. Soon Gopee was selling, collecting the money, and turning it in only for the drugs he could use. Gopee was hooked and going hungry again.

Down Another Rung

One day Gopee was coming down from his last high and realized he was famished. Penniless, he couldn't ask Dude for money. He would just give him another hit "on credit." All he wanted was something to eat. So Gopee ventured to another part of town where young boys and old men met, and quickly he found someone who would buy him some food.

Gopee fell down another rung on the stepladder of life. He became a male prostitute. This is where most young addicts on the streets wind up.

Do we Care?

It's sad but true that today many of our churches don't have a ministry to the homeless and street kids. They are comfortable with their presentable congregations and don't want these down-and-outers contaminating their church.

Often, when conducting special services, I've seen homeless people come in and watched members of the congregation nudge each other and whisper, "What are they doing here?"

We are faced with a Macedonian cry in our churches. People are going to hell and we don't seem concerned. Jesus came and died on Calvary's cross

41

for just such a people.

"For God so loved the world that He gave His only begotten Son, that WHOSOEVER believeth in Him should not perish, but have everlasting life" (John 3:16, emphasis mine).Whosoever means *everyone.*

In reality, we are often the only Jesus street people will ever meet. How do we look and act to them? What would Jesus do? If we don't share the Good News, they will never know there is hope for them in Christ.

"Better" Became Worse

The cycle was complete. Like countless thousands before him who became drug dependent, Gopee just wanted to leave home for something better. What at first appeared to be "better," became worse when obtaining one meal was a whole day's work. Then came the businesses of the street: stealing, drugs and prostitution. The spiral downward was like the final fall of a flaming plane.

The spiral downward was like the final fall of a flaming plane.

Except for a miracle, there would be only fiery destruction coming up fast for Gopee even though he didn't leave home of his own accord.

A New Authority

Many young people run away each year because they don't want to be under parental authority. They complain, "I don't have to do what you tell me, I'm my own boss," and the enticement of the gangs and street seems to be the place to go.

They fail to realize that if they disobey Mom and Dad, the worst thing that can happen is they lose their privileges or their allowance. But, when they get entangled in gangs and drugs, if they don't do what they are told, they may very well lose their life! They may be escaping parental authority, but end up coming under *heavier* authority dictated by the gangs.

"You're Doing What?"

Most of these kids, like Gopee, were unaware hope and help was ready to reach out to them.

There were street ministers who worked where Gopee walked everyday. They stopped and talked to him from time to time. Sometimes Gopee listened, but he always seemed to find some reason to move on. Deep inside he thought Jesus couldn't help a person like him. Dude reinforced Gopee's sense of utter worthlessness.

"You're doing what?" Dude screamed at Gopee. "You're a *#%! whore!"

Dude's fist caught Gopee's chin and spun his small framed body into a crumpled mass. Between the fear and the shock of the blow, he crawled for the exit not ever wanting to be hit that hard again. But then the kicks started coming.

"Don't you crawl away from me you little punk! You want something from me? I'll give it to you!"

Gopee couldn't breathe and passed out.

Wet, cold beer was foaming over Gopee's head and splashed into his mouth. He sat up, coughing blood dregs, and wiping his face. He was still alive, but wishing he wasn't. His eyes were swelling and painful to the touch. His lip was split and throbbing.

He was in agony every time he breathed. Gopee wanted to cry, but he swallowed hard for fear of offending Dude again.

"Look, you gotta bring me the money you make! Just like the girls, I'm gonna be your pimp, see?"

What choice was there? Gopee nodded.

"Get yourself cleaned up and get out of here!"

Again Gopee managed a nod, and started to push himself up. Then Dude put his face into Gopee's, and said, clenching his teeth, "Cross me and I'll kill you, kid. You know what I mean?"

Where Would He Go?

For Gopee, hate and death was personified, and he couldn't speak.

"I said, do you know what I mean?" Dude's hand broadsided Gopee.

"Yes, yes, Dude . . . I know what you mean," Gopee pleaded, "Just don't hit me again, please!"

All other pain shifted to the soaring heat of Dude's slap outlined in pink on Gopee's cheek.

Gopee wanted out, but where would he go, or who would he call? There had to be something better.

7

Who Will Help?

The majority of street people think there is nothing left for them – they are at the end of their rope. This is why it is so vital that we as Christ's representatives do something to help. The churches need to be more involved and sensitive to what kids are up against on the streets. Vulnerable young people are told after they join a gang that they can never escape. But I know from personal experience, with God's help you can!

The Body of Christ needs to assist street ministers and have an open door policy for them to bring the lost souls they work with into the churches. Believers must stop looking at these kids as an *offense* to them.

As I talk to churches across our country, I realize most are clueless concerning street people. They assume all are dirty, smelly, and will steal anything not nailed down. In some cases this is true, yet with the right training and a genuine burden for the lost, the church can be a safe haven and a shelter for many of these bruised, yet valuable kids.

"Riff Raff"

I remember trying to conduct a street crusade in a community where I was supported by the county and the city officials. There was a serious gang and drug problem. I ran ads in the newspaper and on local radio for three weeks inviting pastors and youth ministers to come to a free breakfast on Saturday morning. Only one youth minister showed up!

Desperately wanting to know the reason for the dismal response, I called some of the local churches and asked why they had not attended. Their answer was simple. They didn't want a street crusade because it brought out all the "riff raff" in the area and "We don't want those kind of people in our church."

I believe this attitude derives from fear and not a full understanding of the problem. When we realize these individuals, given half a chance, can be redeemed and productive, many churches are more than willing to offer help in any way they can.

Ask how you can contribute to a street ministry. Not everyone is called into this unique outreach, but everyone can help in some way.

8

"I'll Kill You, Kid!"

"What could be better than this?" Gopee bragged as he talked to the street ministers. "I get by and that's all that matters!"

"That's not all that matters, Gopee! What about God, and your eternal salvation?" the minister asked.

"Hey man, when I don't have to worry about my next meal, then I'll start worrying about eternal salvation!" Gopee smiled.

A New Language

Like a lot of runaways on the streets, Gopee had no idea what the street minister was talking about when he asked, "What about your eternal salvation?" While many people feel called to do this kind of ministry, they need to be taught how to effectively reach street people for Christ.

There are young people who have never heard the

name of God or Jesus, except in profanity. Many have never darkened the door of a church. So, it takes much patience and love to break down the barriers.

You can't wander into these areas and simply announce, "I want to tell you the Good News." They'll ridicule you and ask, "What's that?" You say, "Jesus died for you"? They honestly don't know what you mean. You tell them they need to be washed in the Blood of the Lamb and they think you are crazy!

"You're going to kill a little lamb and wash me in it's blood? Gross!"

You can't wander into these areas and simply announce, "I want to tell you the Good News."

Who knows – some drug-induced kid might try to kill you! Please understand I do not have all the answers, but I just don't want anyone to get hurt trying to lend a helping hand.

"What Happens Then?"

Be compassionate and understand that the people you are dealing with just don't grasp the living truth of the Bible. They, like Gopee, are for the most part longing to find the answer, yet they've been hurt so many times they can't trust anyone. So, with God's help, build the trust by staying the course, like this real-life example:

"Gopee," the minister said in a sincere tone of voice, "I mean what happens if someone beats you up and you don't make it? What happens then? What about heaven and hell?"

"I don't know anything about no heaven and man, we live in hell every day," Gopee said. The minister asked again. "What happens then?"

"Then I guess it's all over! But that ain't gonna happen to me. I'm too fast and I got my gang to front for me," Gopee boasted.

"Suppose you don't make it with your gang." These words struck a nerve. "Then what happens, Gopee?" Many street kids join gangs to feel wanted, not knowing that one simple mistake can cost them their life.

"Aw, man, don't 'dis' me with that jive . . . My gang ain't gonna leave me and I ain't going no where, no how. So just take your religious bull %# *@ and shove it, bro! Know what I mean?"

Dude's clenched teeth flashed in Gopee's mind and he began to sweat with fear.

"Know what I mean?" The words had been hissed by Dude again and again, ending with "I'll kill you, kid!"

Ready to Leave?

Gopee began to seriously think about getting out but that thought could mean death – or at least having the living daylights beaten out of him. The man he was talking to seemed to understand where Gopee was and didn't push the point.

Gopee desperately wanted out! Whatever it took – even if it took God to do it. It sounded like he was finally ready.

9

"Saved From What?"

It was another dismal day for Gopee. He was disappointed with life in general and was, as usual, very hungry. He splashed water in his face, not so much to be clean as to wake himself. If he was to eat, he needed his wits about him.

The same old places and same old faces could still be found. Today, however, everything was a little more dirty and grimy, a little more worn and torn, a lot more *old* and *dying*. And that was just in the first block!

"Man, things are really messed up!" Gopee mumbled to himself. He rubbed his stomach, then the back of his neck. "Next it could be me!" he surmised, shrugging as he headed down the dusty street.

A $300 Habit

On the far corner a friend of his was being

53

hassled by some taller men, but this wasn't uncommon, for she was usually surrounded by men: her pimp, a "john" or two, even a policeman; they were always around her, but she was normally in control.

This time she *wasn't* in charge, and these two men seemed to be bothering her. On the streets you move in cautiously because things aren't always as they appear. Gopee was anxious, but definitely believed in self-preservation. He walked steadily toward his friend, (well, not exactly a friend but a close acquaintance) and acted disinterested in the grouping.

"I'm 13 years old. I've been a hooker since I was 11"

A few feet from the men, Gopee stopped to adjust his gym shoes. He sat back on the cement steps to take in the sunshine and conveniently hear what was going on.

"You don't understand," she pleaded. "I'm 13 years old. I've been a hooker since I was 11. I've got a $300-a-day habit, and you say there's a way out? Are you gonna pay my habit?"

"Yes, there is a way out of drugs and prostitution. His Name is Jesus. He says in John 14:6, *"I am the way, the truth and the life. No one comes to the Father except through me"*(NIV).

Then one of the men spoke words that caught Gopee's attention. He explained how the Bible states in Acts 2:21, *"Everyone who calls on the name of the Lord will be saved"*(NIV).

"We're All the Same"

Gopee thought, "Saved! Saved from what?" His thoughts were cut short when he heard his friend exclaim, "But He can't save me!" She started to cry. "I'll never be any good," she sobbed.

"There is 'Good News' for all of us," the Church worker continued. "The Bible says in Romans 3:10, "There is no one righteous, no not one." So we're all the same. In fact, Jesus met a woman who was caught in the very act of adultery – and some people wanted to harm her. Jesus calmly said, 'Let him who is without sin, let him cast the first stone . . .' No one stepped forward."

He continued, "In fact, God promises, 'Come let us reason together, though your sins be like scarlet, they shall be white as snow . . .' All you need to do is ask God to forgive your sins in the Name of Jesus Christ, and He will. Not because I ask you to, but because the Bible says so. 1 John 1:9 tells us: 'If we confess our sins, he is faithful and just to forgive our sins, and cleanse us from all unrighteousness'"

Then the man added, "And I know He'll do it

because He did it for me!

"Really? How?" the young girl questioned.

A New Kind of Drug?

The man told her his life story as she listened with open eyes and ears. Gopee, not realizing it, was listening too. The girl asked the man if Jesus could forgive her for all the things she had done. The man gently smiled and quoted John 3:16: "For God so loved the world, that He gave His only begotten Son, that whosoever believeth in Him should not perish, but have everlasting life."

Right there, on a filthy sidewalk, the young prostitute asked Jesus to forgive her sins.

The two men began to cry and laugh at the same time. The young girl joined in, crying and laughing with them.

Gopee sat watching the two men and his friend, thinking, "This is crazy, this must be a new kind of drug or something. You cry when you are sad and laugh when you're happy But they're doing both at the same time!"

Gopee's first thoughts were, "Man, if I can get some of this, I could sell it and it would bring a good price."

56

What Does it Mean?

As he continued eavesdropping on their conversation, they talked about going to church and being baptized. Gopee didn't know what they meant, but thought it must be something you get high on. No one can laugh and cry at the same time unless you're buzzing on some drug. He tried to remember the last time he laughed out loud. But he could only recall the bad times. Yet it didn't look like they were doing anything other than just talking. What was that all about?

This was all new to Gopee.

> *Forgiveness, grace, hope – these were foreign concepts to Gopee.*

Crying over so many words that didn't hurt or really make sense to him? Forgiveness, grace, hope – these were foreign concepts to Gopee. Hard cash, drugs, a plate of food, now these were terms he understood. If you wanted to get clean, then you took a bath. He guessed that if you wanted to get eternally clean, then you took an *eternal* bath!

Finally, a Smile

For the first time in a long while, Gopee smiled as

he pictured himself in a huge sudsy bathtub floating high in the clouds. It was almost worth thinking about: to be that squeaky clean.

Gopee was beaming without realizing it. Here he was, splashing, making bubble-beads, and becoming pleasantly wrinkled in the warm water. It was reminiscent of the times his father gave him a bath. With that thought still lingering in his mind, his father appeared with a towel, smiling, ready for Gopee to get out of the tub.

"My father .." Gopee gasped as the vision dissolved into the open street scene. "My father . . ." Gopee repeated.

He couldn't catch the connection. He scratched his head wondering, but then hunger overtook his wandering thoughts. Behind him the street-workers and the forgiven prostitute were hugging and leaving together.

10

Gasping for Breath!

Six months had passed and Gopee never really missed the girl. Like so many others who came and went on the streets, if you didn't see them you didn't have to deal with them– or the pain of their loss.

Death came many times to familiar faces. After a while, even the young eyes of Gopee saw more than a lifetime of dead and dying men, women, boys and girls. They were too close to being like himself to dwell on it. It was depressing – and depression rode on the shoulders of every druggie.

One look back and it was a sheer drop to the emotional ruins of regret. Gopee tried to never look behind him. That way it was tolerable.

Broken Thoughts

An old oak growing in front of the gang's house let Gopee lean on it as he appraised his life. There was the gang and Dude. He had a place to sleep where it was warm in the winter. Yeah, so there were six others in the room and it smelled like dirty feet, but at least he belonged somewhere. Someday he'd get a place of his own and wouldn't have to share one of the three mattresses, or fight for one of the two folding chairs.

He laid his head back, thinking of his future alone, and mentally outfitted his own apartment. However, his thoughts were broken by a loud voice.

"You stupid deaf kid!" A large hand shook Gopee. "I've been yelling your dumb name for five minutes!" He paused, letting him go. "Dude wants you... NOW!"

A large hand shook Gopee. "I've been yelling your dumb name for five minutes!"

Nothing Seemed to Fit

Obediently, Gopee fell in behind Bear, Dude's lieutenant. Bear was always pawing on Gopee. He was homosexual, and Gopee had rejected him more than once. It was strange that Bear let go of him so quickly, for he usually enjoyed any excuse to hold on.

Maybe things were changing. Perhaps Dude was finally realizing he needed someone like himself.

Yeah, that was it! Dude needed him and he needed Dude.

"NOW Gopee, not tomorrow!" Dude bellowed from his office. Gopee could tell by the tone of Dude's voice he was upset.

Bear stood at the door with his arms crossing his six foot four inch frame. He was 20 years old, but like most body guards looked much older. He just peered down at Gopee and smiled. As Gopee passed, the smile became a muffled laugh.

Strangely, the gruff voice didn't fit this relaxed scene – nothing seemed to fit.

Dude was reclining with his boots up on the old familiar desk and his hands patting his prized belt buckle. Strangely, the gruff voice didn't fit this relaxed scene – *nothing* seemed to fit. The old couch with the exposed spring didn't fit with the image of the well-dressed Dude. The wildness in Dude's eyes didn't fit with his relaxed position either, but his mood would change quickly enough.

Why Was Dude Upset?

"You wanted to see me, Dude?" Gopee asked as he stopped close to the desk.

Bear had followed Gopee across the room, continuing around to Dude's side. Dude glanced up at Bear, and smiled lazily.

It was then that Gopee started guessing that Dude was "high" onr something. The mirror on the desk and new razor blade had a telltale white dusting. 'Coke?' Gopee wondered what side of Dude's personality he would be talking to. Bear smiled down at Dude, his arms still crossed in the "body guard" pose.

Gopee's heart began to beat faster, sensing something bad was about to happen.

"Maybe it will be all right?" Gopee hoped. He didn't know that along with the coke, Dude had also done some "angel dust." He was wired! Gopee's heart began to beat faster, sensing something bad was about to happen.

Dude moved his boots from the desktop, and quickly sat up in the creaking chair. Bear began to stare intently at Gopee. Unsettling as this was, Dude rose from his chair with a broad smile.

The Taste of Blood

Gopee relaxed. Dude was in charge so he had nothing to fear. This was his everyday hero. Dude

62

was as close to a father as Gopee had known since he left home. Secretly, Gopee enjoyed it when this man would put his arm around him to talk. So Gopee smiled broadly when Dude started to hug him close.

Then the hug tightened into a neck hold. Gopee had to breathe and the smell of an armpit was filtering the air. It was unpleasant at best, but Gopee couldn't move.

"Gopee, my boy, haven't I been good to you?" Dude said, "I give you a nice place to stay, don't I?"

Gopee nodded as best he could, adding "Yeah, Dude . . .why?"

"Gopee, my boy, haven't I been good to you?" Dude said, "I give you a nice place to stay, don't I?"

"Well, " Dude interjected, "What do you think should happen to a lying . . . stealing . . . little %#$! that would steal from someone who took them in and gave them a roof over their head . . . and food . . . and really loved them . . . and showed them the 'good life' . . . and then they go and steal from them?"

Dude's hold on Gopee tightened with each point he made. By now Gopee wasn't breathing that easily, and fear was all over him. "I don't know, Dude?" Gopee gulped for air, "Why? . . ."

Pain seared through Gopee's neck as Dude slung him around to meet him eye to eye, and Dude screamed in his face, "You . . . you little %#!$ . . . you're the one who stole $30 from me!"

Again, intense pain. This time it was Gopee's nose and face. The taste of blood was immediate and a warm stream rolled over his swelling face, spotting bright red on the dirty floor.

The taste of blood was immediate and a warm stream rolled over his swelling face, spotting bright red on the dirty floor.

Before Gopee could react, Dude grabbed his neck and squeezed tight. Tears and blood further blocked Gopee's airway, and he could only claw at Dude's hand to let some air pass to his lungs. Dude, along with Bear, worked out with weights. Gopee's 90 pounds was almost one arm-press for Dude.

The Door Slammed!

Gopee held onto Dude's squeezing grip, gasping for air. He felt himself being lifted and then his legs swinging free. Pain again; this time Gopee's left eye blazed.

The blow knocked all consciousness from him

and he crumpled awkwardly like so much trash on the dirty floor. Dude motioned with his head for Bear to leave with him, but Bear couldn't resist adding a kick to Gopee's stomach. He sighed unconsciously as the remaining air left his lungs. The door slammed shut amid the drug-laced laughs of Dude and Bear.

Then there was silence.

11

A Soothing Touch

Gopee woke to excruciating pain in his face and body. He tried to breathe without agony, but couldn't. His stomach hurt. He tried to move, but that hurt too. His left eye was swelling and was almost shut. He needed help, but the pain kept him from calling out. Then there were sounds at the door. Perhaps someone was coming to his aid.

"Is that little %#@! . . . still here?" Dude, Bear, and the entire gang circled around Gopee.

Through his one eye, Gopee could see them staring at him. They were all smiling and laughing their approval at what they saw. A couple of the gang even clapped.

Dude reached down to Gopee's midsection and yanked, bellowing, "I want you to see what happens to a lying punk that steals from 'the Dude.'"

Amid Gopee's groans, Dude growled, "I ought to cut off the rest of your fingers, you worthless little turd!"

Dude dropped Gopee to the floor, raised his boot

over Gopee's right hand, and stomped with all his weight.

He was now in shock, hardly feeling the surge of new pain. For Dude and most of the gang, it was time to leave. But for Bear and the other two homosexuals, their fun with Gopee was just beginning. He couldn't move or resist.

For about two hours, Gopee was abused and raped. Finally, he was left to himself.

"Cat" Wanted to Help

The door creaked again. Another tormentor? Gopee closed his one good eye and waited. What else could he do?

"Oh, Gopee!" The quiet voice of "Cat" whispered to him.

This was the only friend Gopee had, a 13-year old prostitute – one of many he knew. Cat belonged to the gang, but still she wanted to help Gopee.

He opened his right eye and saw Cat's concern. She helped him up to the couch and covered him. Gopee was embarrassed, and grateful at the same time.

Cat truly liked Gopee, and she couldn't hold back the tears as she wiped the blood from his face. He tolerated the pain he felt with each wipe, because the coolness of the water and her gentle touch was so

68

soothing. Soon, Gopee fell asleep.

Cat finished the last swabs of Gopee's face, taking inventory of his wounds. His eye was swollen shut, his nose was cut and his hand was doubled in size. For now it was best to let him sleep. As she carefully settled back on the couch, she began to think of her own wounds and why she was even there.

Cat finished the last swabs of Gopee's face, taking inventory of his wounds.

"See Ya!"

Cat came from a nice home and a Christian family. But at school, she fell in with the "party crowd."

With her Mom always busy with activities at the church and her Dad either at the office or on the golf course, she was left to entertain herself quite frequently.

"Cat, here's a few dollars for the movies," her Mom would say, "Just be back at a decent hour and make sure you enjoy yourself . . . Now give me a kiss, and wish your Dad and me a good time."

"Have a good time, Mom," she said, as always. Then she added, "Mom, I sure wish we could *all* go to the movies."

"Oh, we will, sometime soon, honey. Just not tonight." Her Dad chimed in. "We'll try next week, okay?"

If they couldn't spare the time for her, she would certainly find something better to do with their money.

"Not next week, remember that's the church social," Mom reminded them both.

"Oh, yeah, " Dad thought out loud, "but we'll get together soon! Come on or we'll be late!"

"See, ya!" Dad followed dutifully out with his wife.

It was one of the last times they saw Cat. As an only child, she felt more and more like a burden. If they couldn't spare the time for her, she would certainly find something better to do with their money.

No Time

Today, most parents are so caught up in the rat-race of life, they don't carve out time for their kids. They drop them off at school or put them on the bus and feel their obligation is over. They work night and day – trying to make money to give their kids what they didn't have. When you drive by their house you see a new boat, camper, pickup truck, and a motorcycle, none of which their children are old enough to enjoy.

As parents we are often guilty of using our children as an excuse to accumulate things *we* want, not treasuring the most precious commodity we will ever have – our sons and daughters. Instead of giving them what we *didn't* have, why don't we give them what most children are raised with: good morals, high standards, and quality time together as a family.

The average parent today spends about five and a half minutes a day with their children, while television spends 27.8 hours a week with them – and before they leave elementary school they have witnessed twenty thousand murders and one hundred thousand assaults.

No wonder so many kids are in trouble. And when tragedy strikes, the parents often try to blame it on each other.

"I Can't Take It!"

This sounds like the conversation between Cat's parents at the police station that night. "You could have spent a little more time with her than with your golfing buddies." Cat's Mom rubbed her forehead as she pushed her husband from the front seat of the car.

"Me? Look, it was your responsibility to be with

her when I had to see my clients on the golf course," he retorted.

"My responsibility!" she exclaimed. "We *both* have obligations. You with your work and me with mine."

"Well, what work do you do?" Dad broke in.

"What do you mean by that comment?" her eyes glared back. "Who is it that makes sure those wives are happy while you men play your golf?"

"Look, she's your daughter, can't you control her?" Dad lost it and began cursing!

It was always like this, Cat thought. Here she was sick to her stomach and coming down fast from the high she was on, while her parents only cared about blaming each other. She began to sob.

"This is just too much for me! I can't take it anymore!" said her Mom. Her words stabbed at Cat's heart with overwhelming sadness.

If her parents couldn't help Cat as an only child, then she would relieve them of the burden. Her mind was made up, she would be gone before they knew what happened.

12

Searching for Love

The gang members were hitting on Cat continuously, like they did all the girls. Offers of free drugs and good times, though refused in the past, captivated her now.

It began when she made a phone call to a friend.

"Yeah, who's this," the voice was Jim's but more gruff than usual.

Meekly, Cat responded, "It's Cat."

Jim's voice quickly changed to warmth. "Cat . . . Cat . . . you really surprised me by calling. Jim recovered from the surprise of hearing her voice. "It's nice to hear from you."

"Thanks," she hesitated, then plunged ahead, "Jim, your offer is still good . . . right?"

"Offer? Offer of what?" he asked cautiously. Jim was making sure.

"You know . . . the drugs and . . . and a good time!" Cat closed her eyes as she said the last part.

"Cat, are you all right?" Jim's words were the first concern she had heard in quite awhile. They moved from her mind and settled in her heart. Within moments, Jim was picking up Cat at the phone booth. Then they were drinking coffee together and she told him her story.

Sleepless Nights

"My Old Man and Old Lady did the same thing to me when I got in trouble," Jim said, "only they told me to get out. Man, I left that night and joined up with Dude and the gang." Jim smiled, "Now, I've got it made." He paused, and looked directly into Cat's eyes and slowed down a little, "Why don't you become my Ol' Lady and join with us, Cat? Then, you wouldn't have to take any crap from anyone. What do you say, Cat?"

Jim held onto her hand lovingly. She nodded and that night left her family for the acceptance of the gang.

She was 13 now, and even though a couple years had passed, drugs and alcohol had aged Cat. Because of her drug habit, she was a prostitute. Sleepless nights helped take a further toll on her youth. Only make-up helped to hide the age lines. When she cried it smeared and ran – just as it was doing now.

"I Have a Gang to Run"

Gopee was also crying, asking Cat why Dude had beat him to a pulp. "I didn't steal any money."

"Dude was high, Gopee," she said, "and wanted to feel big and prove he was the boss, that's all."

Gopee sighed and fell asleep 'til the next morning. Again, he tried to move, but he hurt too much. He also wanted to leave, but the pain kept him on the sofa. Breathing was an effort, and the incessant pain made him want to die.

"Awake, finally!" Dude said, leaning against the doorway. He pushed himself erect and walked to the sofa. Instinctively, Gopee held his breath as Dude passed him.

Dude stopped, grabbed a folding chair and sat down.

Breathing was an effort, and the incessant pain made him want to die.

"You know," Speaking softly, he began, "I'm really sorry about having to hurt you like this. But you understand I have a gang to run." He turned to Bear who had taken Dude's position in the doorway, and smiled, "I've got to show these punks who's boss, Gopee."

He leaned into Gopee, and said quietly. "I really like you . . . Heck man, I love you, Gopee. Dude sat back, "I figured that if I showed the gang I would beat the hell out of you, then they'd know that I'd kill them too."

He looked over at Bear and then back to Gopee, whispering, "Look, Bear and his buddies were just . . . having a little fun with you." Dude smiled, "You know, old pal, I'll take care of you, and you're going to be my right hand man one day. By the way, that little %#@& Cat that cleaned you up. Man, don't mess with her. She's HIV positive. The #$@! is going to die with AIDS."

Dude and Bear laughed leaving the room together. Dude glanced back at Gopee and slapped Bear's shoulders, laughing once more. Then the door slammed shut into silence.

His Mind Drifted

Cat was the only friend Gopee had. The thought of her having AIDS and him losing her was hard to digest. But his mind snapped back to what Dude had said, taking away the depressing thought of Cat's problem.

"Dude's right hand man!" Gopee whispered his thoughts out loud. All he could think about was pleasing Dude. Since he had been on the streets, no one else had ever showed him any kindness.

His mind drifted back to his home. Gopee wished

his life could have remained like it was when his Mom and Dad were together. He remembered how they used to play games in the park on Sunday afternoon. As a small child, he would go shopping with his Mom. Saturdays meant fishing with his Dad.

IT HAPPENED TO ME

Today we have so many single parents – many a product of divorce. Why can't we, as adults, stop placing blame on each other and think of the children that are caught in the middle of these break-ups? They didn't ask to be born, but they are with us now.

Parents, start being a parent, not looking for an excuse for your shortcomings. We all have them. Spend time with your child (or children). It can help build character in them even if you and your spouse can't get along.

Parents, start being a parent, not looking for an excuse for your shortcomings.

"No, Dad!"

I remember when my wife was killed leaving me with four children. I tried to shower them with everything they wanted thinking that would demonstrate how much I loved them. But I found out the hard way it was time together they really craved.

Each of my kids received a new car on their sixteenth birthday. When my son, Eddie, turned 16, I did just that, only to find out three days later he had been arrested for possession with the intent to distribute. I bailed him out of jail and when we arrived home I sat him down at the kitchen table and, with my finger in his face said, "Eddie, haven't I given you everything you ever wanted? Why did you do this to me?"

> *"Eddie, haven't I given you everything you ever wanted? Why did you do this to me?"*

He raised up and looked me right in my eyes, pointed his finger in my face and replied, "No, Dad! You gave me everything you thought I wanted. But the one thing I really needed, Dad, you were to busy to give me."

"What is that?" I asked.

"You, Dad! You."

On the River

The reality of my lifestyle hit home. I had made sure my children were given all the material possessions and participated in all the activities kids want to do, but I always sent them with someone else, not *me!*

Suddenly I realized I was looking at a very angry young man. Eddie liked to trout fish, so I asked, "Son, do you think it's too late for us?"

"I don't know, Dad," he replied. I asked him if we could go trout fishing that weekend. He said, "Yeah, I guess so."

We went to the river and it was the worst weekend of my life! Eddie caught every rock *in* the river and every limb *over* the river. On the way home we didn't do much talking. But about five miles from the house, Eddie looked over at me and said, "Dad, do you think we could do this again next weekend?"

I have to admit, every fiber of my being was screaming with deafening tones, NO WAY! Yet when I spoke it came out of my mouth as "Okay, sure."

We returned the next weekend and we had the most precious time a father and son could possibly have. Eddie came up to me in the middle of the river, put his arm around me and said, "Dad, I love you. Thanks for being my dad."

I put my arms around him and we were standing there hugging, crying and laughing.

"You Should be Ashamed!"

By now, there was quite a crowd gathering on the bank and bridge wondering what these two guys were doing as we embraced each other in view of everybody. As we climbed the bank, there were people taking pictures and one lady commented, "You should be ashamed!"

I replied, "I am, lady, but not for the reason you think. This is my son, and I love him." Eddie looked at her and said, "Yeah, man, this is my Dad!"

In three months my son changed his friends and went back to school. I didn't even know he had dropped out!

Today, he is the father of three lovely girls and he and his wife spend all the time they can together as a family. And we still go fishing quite often.

GOPEE CLOSED HIS EYES

"Man, would I like to go fishing again . . . ohhhhh!" Gopee's thoughts dissolved into pain where Bear had kicked him. Painful reality said Gopee could never go back and that he was trapped where he was forever. Somehow, though, thoughts of God and Jesus began to wander into Gopee's mind.

"Those people at church . . . always talking about this man named Jesus." The pictures of these clean, well-dressed people seemed like his Mom and Dad, but they didn't come to his neighborhood.

"Oh well, there ain't no God," Gopee said doubtfully. "Even if He is alive, He don't live in my 'hood. All He wants are those good people in church. He wouldn't have anything to do with the likes of me!"

Gopee coughed in pain. "God's not real! But this pain sure is!"

He closed his eyes and tried to sleep.

13

"I Don't Want Him"

About two weeks later, Gopee received news that broke his heart. "Gopee! Gopee!" Dude barked from his desk in the other room. "Good to see you pal," Dude smirked at the others in the room, then sat up with a false look of concern.

"Gopee, I'm afraid I got bad news for you. It's your girlfriend, Cat." Dude suppressed a grin, then said, "She OD'd, man. That Crack freak is gone!"

Then Dude smiled mockingly, "Sorry, Gopee." He was waiting for him to cry in front of them, but Gopee didn't oblige. He showed no emotion, because by now he had no feelings.

"Don't take it so hard man!" Dude knew what Gopee must have been thinking. "She wasn't any good anyway!" Dude was on his way out with the others, "Right, Bro?" Dude's closed fist met Bear's who returned with, "That's right!" Their laughs followed them out and faded to muffled sounds when the door slammed.

Gopee watched them leave through Dude's "office" window. A hard knot formed in his throat, and headed down toward his heart. There it seemed to tighten like his own fist until there wasn't anymore feeling. Before he knew it, Gopee was back on the street headed to his next drug deal.

A hard knot formed in his throat, and headed down to his heart.

"What's Your Name?"

He almost didn't see the boy in the alley. His large fearful eyes were what stopped Gopee.

"Hey, you!" Gopee said, his tough street voice startling the boy. "What you doin' in there?" A sense of power and control surged through Gopee as he approached the boy. He could see the fear he evoked. He could almost smell it: "What's your name?"

"Bob," his voice quivered.

Gopee studied his face, then asked, "Well, Bob, where you from?"

"I ran away from home," then added reasons for his leaving. "My parents argue and fight all the time . . . I'm fed up with it." Then Bob, diverting his eyes to the sidewalk, said, "I think they always fight because of me!"

Gopee understood too well without admitting it. Perhaps they could be friends, he thought. "Bob," Gopee used a friendlier tone, "I'm gonna make some money. You wanna come along?"

Bob looked up and smiled broadly, "Yeah!"

Gopee shortened his normal stride to that of his new friend. Somehow "Bob" was too plain a name for him.

"I'm gonna have to find you a better street name than Bob." Within the swirl of friendly memories, Cat's name came to mind.

"I know. I had a friend named Cat once. I'll call you Bob-Cat, in memory of her! Okay?"

Bob, now Bob-Cat smiled, nodded, and then noticed Gopee's hand. Three fingernails were still blackened from Dude's boot heel stomping his right hand. Bob-Cat winced, and asked, "Man, how did you mash your hand?"

Gopee didn't want to scare Bob-Cat off from meeting Dude, that would happen soon enough.

"Oh, the hand . . . car door!" Gopee saw Bob-Cat grimace and motioning with his other hand, quickened the pace so that they didn't talk any more until the drugs were delivered.

Dude Was Mad!

Afterwards, Gopee wasn't sure if he should bring

his new friend to meet Dude or not. Bob-Cat had no place to go, so the house was the only choice. As they approached the steps, Dude stood in the doorway. The stark light of the hallway kept Gopee from seeing Dude's expression until it was too late.

Dude was mad! Gopee knew from the pit of his stomach there was trouble. Dude snarled, "Who's this with you?"

Bob spoke before Gopee could stop him, "My name's Bob-Cat. Gopee's my new friend. He gave me my name."

Bob-Cat's innocent smile looked over for approval from Gopee. But "pride of ownership" is a short-lived commodity on the streets, and especially around Dude.

Dude bent his head so he could peer over the rims of his sunglasses. Gopee could see the eyebrows close in a maddening "V" shape. He wanted to tell Bob-Cat to run, but the words wouldn't form in his mouth. Bob-Cat's face was almost radiant with pride in his new found friend.

"Please, Stop!"

The smack of Dude's backhand wheeled Bob-Cat toward the street and Dude stood up, towering over Gopee and his bleeding friend. Dude leaned down into Gopee's face, "Oh, so you're finding members now are ya?"

"No, Dude," Gopee replied, "I . . . I just wanted a friend." Gopee reached for Bob-Cat's shoulder, but he winced and pulled away. "You didn't have to hit him like that!" Gopee glared back at Dude.

"Oh, really?" Dude stepped forward and caught Gopee in the stomach, lifting him off the small porch. Dude strode again and readied himself for another kick, but his leg wouldn't move. It was Bob-Cat protecting it. "Stop . . . stop . . . stop . . . Please, stop!" Bob-Cat hung onto Dude's leg, yelling with his eyes closed.

By this time, Bear heard the commotion and peeled Bob-Cat from Dude's leg, all the while Bob-Cat continued to yell. It wasn't until he was lifted eye-to-eye with Bear that he stopped screaming.

"This one of yours?" Bear smiled at Dude.

"No, " Dude snarled, "you can have the little fart! I don't want him.

14

Pushing the Boundaries

Bob-Cat may have stopped yelling, yet the squirming and kicking to get loose never ended. Bear was too strong, but still it took two of his friends to take him into the house.

Gopee began to plead for his new pal. Dude just laughed, "You brought him here. Now they're just initiating him into the gang." Dude turned his back on Gopee.

Gopee had nothing but hate for Dude now. His unprotected back would make an easy target, he thought. One shot, one blow to his head, one stab and his problems would go away forever!

Gopee watched Dude as he picked up his sunglasses, smoothed his hair, and walked up the stairs. Dude glanced back and smiled, then disappeared into the house.

Gopee knew something awful happened to Bob-Cat, but he never saw him again. "Mind your own business!" Bear's finger punctuated each syllable of the short sentence. Bear turned and smiled knowingly to his friends. Gopee rubbed his chest absentmindedly.

"I don't have to be a part of this gang. " Gopee muttered to himself. He was 15 years old now. Although he was young, he had seen enough to start his own gang, or at least try to get out of this one.

Gopee never really found out what happened to his friend Bob-Cat. One of the gang members told him they (Bear and a couple of the other members) abused him all night and then took him fishing. Gopee knew what that meant, but he could never prove it.

"We're Having a Ball!"

He began to spend time by himself and go outside his territory. It was dangerous to venture out of your own turf, but now Gopee, disillusioned, was willing to take the risk.

He wandered further and further. This day he saw kids talking to some men who looked like biker-types, only cleaner somehow. Curious, Gopee tried to get close enough to hear as one of the men looked up. "Say man, why don't you come over. We're having a ball!"

"Yeah, sure," Gopee nodded and was about to

turn away.

"We're talking about Jesus" the man said.

Gopee was startled enough to shout back, "There ain't no Jesus, and there certainly ain't no God!"

He felt so justified, so invincible. But now, the man was moving toward him. Immediately, Gopee felt guilty and defenseless. He wanted to run, but couldn't. The man's smile was compelling him to stay.

"Here, let me give you this and invite you to come tonight to a rally we're having."

Without thinking, Gopee took the booklet. Finally, he weakly objected, "I . . . I can't come to no rally . . . I got to work!"

Gopee felt guilty and defenseless. He wanted to run, but couldn't.

"Work?" the man almost laughed, but stifled it for this young boy's sake, "You're not old enough to work!"

"I'm older than you think," Gopee tried to say in his harshest voice. "I got a job!"

"A Man Like Me"

Gopee's angry response just made the man smile broader, but then he said more seriously, "I'm sorry. I didn't mean to make you mad. It's just . . . I was surprised to hear a man like you had a job."

"A man like me," – Gopee enjoyed that. It was the first time anyone ever called him a man.

"Hey, what's your name?" this smiling biker inquired.

Giving him his full attention, he said, "My name's Gopee."

For the man, his memory searched still-frame images until the breakfast meeting of the two was recalled. Then, like a videotape, the scene played out and ended as Gopee walked away.

Torn Into Pieces

"I need someone to read this to me," he thought aloud. "Maybe someone in the gang will."

For Gopee, he never felt better about himself. It took some time for the good feeling to dissipate. Until then Gopee had forgotten about the booklet tucked in his pocket. He looked at it now. The pictures were okay, but he could barely read. "I need someone to read this to me," he thought aloud. "Maybe someone in the gang will!"

If Gopee had known what the booklet contained, he would have never taken it back to the house.

"Hey, read this to me," Gopee asked a boy everyone called Dog.

Surprisingly, Dog obliged and read it to him. Dog was 18, and joined the gang about a year earlier. Like everyone else, he was always trying to impress Dude.

"Where'd ya get this?" Dog wanted to know.

On the streets, information was worth money, food, and with the right information with the wrong person, perhaps it was worth your life.

> *"Where'd ya get this?" Dog wanted to know.*

For a moment, Gopee was thinking about the booklet, and forgot to guard its source as he told Dog where it came from.

"That's outside our territory. Hey, Dude, did you know Gopee's been going outside our turf?" Dog yelled as he brushed past Gopee into Dude's office.

There, Dude took the booklet . . . the tract . . . read it briefly, laughed and tore it into the smallest pieces he could. "If I ever find out you've been hanging around those flakes up there again, I'll beat you worse than I did the last time. You hear me, you little snot?"

Dude took a deep breath and began again, "I don't want them Jesus freaks talking to any of my people. They start trouble by telling everyone about Jesus forgiving them for everything they have ever done."

Dude stopped, as if he was remembering a past encounter with "these people" and didn't realize he had just preached a good message.

Staring at the Ceiling

Gopee thought of the young prostitute who asked Jesus to forgive her that day on the street. He knew he had made Dude mad, but the memory remained in his mind.

> "Maybe there is something to this Jesus after all," Gopee thought.

"Maybe there is something to this Jesus after all," Gopee thought – especially if it upset Dude so much. That night, Gopee decided to sleep at the house. He had a lot to mull over and was in no mood to go out with the other gang members or find some other place to rest his weary body.

Gopee would later find out this might have saved his life on two accounts. First, a car accident killed three of the five gang members who were high on drugs. Second, Dude ordered Bear to watch Gopee.

So he just went to his dirty old room and laid down to sleep. He stared at the ceiling thinking about Dude's comments concerning Jesus, and how friendly the man was who gave him the tract.

Gopee was interested in learning more from this individual, but with the thought of Dude finding out, he numbly traced the impression of Dude's boot heel on his hand and remembered the pain.

That was the last thing on Gopee's mind before he awoke the next morning.

15

"Got a Few Minutes to Talk?"

It was Sunday, a good day for a walk, Gopee decided. But what direction should he take?

He decided that the center of town was the place to go, and turned the corner. Although everything looked familiar, things were different somehow, like an unseen hand was drawing him along. Not knowing what it was, Gopee kept walking until he rounded a corner near a church.

Bells rang out, startling him for a moment. Sure he had heard them before, but never this close. He could almost feel the vibrations of the sound they made. He strolled a little closer and watched people getting out of their cars to go into the church. Kids his age were all dressed up, clean as a whistle, headed inside with their parents.

"What a bunch of nerds," Gopee commented to himself. "Look at 'em. All new shoes . . . clothes . . .

and their hair all fixed up. What a bunch of sissies."

Gopee would have gone in himself, but the man with the tract walked toward the church's entrance. It was the same man Dude didn't like who caused so much trouble.

Gopee ducked down behind a car. He didn't want to be seen by the man as he walked into the church. Gopee sighed in relief that Dude wouldn't find him in no "church." He was safe – or so he thought.

Ashamed and Embarrassed

Up the street, some kids he knew invited Gopee to "fool around" for awhile. They stopped to talk and the conversation turned to school and their homes. Gopee had nothing to offer on this topic, so he retraced his steps back to the house. Little did Gopee know that as he would pass by the church, the doors would fling open.

People just seemed to stream out from every doorway. Gopee was engulfed with well dressed people all around him.

"My Lord, look at that!" One of them pointed to Gopee. "That's what's wrong with our kids today. His mother ought to be ashamed of herself letting him out looking like that!"

Another commented, "I'd sure hate to have that family in our church," he said, touching his nose.

Then, they both chuckled, assuring themselves that the ushers would deal with the situation if they tried to enter the church. Gopee hung his head, completely ashamed and embarrassed.

"I don't want to go to their church anyway," he began to console himself. "They're all a bunch of stuck up so and so's."

"Hey, Old Pal"

Gopee raised his head again, but before he could utter another word, the man with the tract was coming out of the church headed straight for him.

"Hey, old pal, how are things going?" He smiled broadly at Gopee.

"I don't need you or your fancy dressed church, so stay away and leave me alone!"

"I'm not your 'old pal'," Gopee retorted, "but things are going just fine. I don't need you or your fancy dressed church, so stay away and leave me alone!"

Gopee raised his voice so others could hear. "I know how you folks feel about people like me!" The man could see the hurt, yet he continued to smile.

"Jesus loves you just the way you are," he said, "and so do I!"

Gopee was stunned. No one ever told him that Jesus – or anyone – loved him like that. But then Gopee snapped back, "Yeah sure, then why did them people say they didn't want me in their precious church . . . Admit it, you don't either."

The man just kept on smiling, "Heck, they don't want me in there either. I was just invited to speak. I attend a small church outside of town, and we don't care how you dress, just as long as you come to worship Jesus.

Curiosity rose up in Gopee, "What do you mean, 'worship Jesus'?"

"Got a few minutes to talk?" the man asked.

Gopee looked around for any gang members and not seeing any, replied, "I might have a minute."

"Well, good." The guest speaker put his arm around Gopee's shoulders and they began to walk together toward a fountain in front of the church.

Gopee Could Relate

The fountain was beautiful to Gopee. The water was sparkling clear with goldfish swimming in the pool. A small white bench was just large enough for the two of them to sit comfortably. Gopee listened attentively as the gentleman shared the story of his life.

Gopee found out that the man was about 12 when

he, too, ran away from home and joined a street gang. By 14, he had his own gang and a string of prostitutes. His boys would steal and sell drugs, and the gang would wait in an alley while one of the smallest would yell names and make gestures to the passing cars, daring them to stop. When the drivers did halt, and chase him into the alley, the other gang members would rob them and strip the car.

This impressed Gopee, who listened with rapt attention to how this man ran his operation.

> *"I beat up anyone in the gang who didn't follow my rules."*

"I beat up anyone in the gang who didn't follow my rules," he said. Gopee could relate to that, but he noticed the man seemed to lower his head just then.

A Nobody!

Gopee decided he needed to perk up the conversation, "That's what I'm going to do someday!"

"What's that?" the man asked.

"Have my very own gang," Gopee smiled proudly, "and then I'll show the world I'm really somebody." Then he folded his arms around himself with a self-satisfied grin.

Tears welled up in the gentleman's eyes, "Son . . . I used to think I was somebody when I ran the gang. But I soon found out I was *nobody*. No matter how much money I accumulated, or how much power I had, I was a nobody."

Looking straight at Gopee, he continued, "You see son, I grew up and moved on into bigger gangs and larger operations. I became very rich selling drugs and running prostitutes."

"When I had a lot of money, I discovered I didn't have one friend in the world."

He took a breath, "But when I had a lot of money, I discovered I didn't have one friend in the world. Everybody I knew wanted my position and my cash, and would kill me to get it."

"But I thought if you had money, you would be happy." Gopee interrupted.

"Son, when I was a millionaire, I was the most unhappy person in the world," he said as he laughed. "I was seeing two head-shrinkers twice a week."

Even Gopee had to laugh, "Why?"

That brought a small pause from the man. Then he said, "Well, I needed someone to talk to . . . to be my friend. But they weren't my pals. They just wanted the hundred dollars an hour I was paying them!"

He added, "You see, Gopee, I couldn't have any friends. If I did, my enemies would use *them* to get *me.*"

The Big Gang!

He turned, staring into space as if he was remembering something and then looking back at Gopee admitted, "I've been shot twice, stabbed many times, and two of my homes were burned to the ground. My son was kidnaped, and my wife . . ." he paused again, "my wife was murdered!"

He went on to explain, "I spent 15 years in organized crime, advancing from a street gang into the *big* gang. I ran a five-state prostitution ring with over three hundred girls working for me." Gopee's eyes grew bigger as the conversation continued.

"Later, I had the opportunity to take over a drug operation and I made some people real mad. I was shot in the back by a so-called friend and was taken to a hospital. They called my parents who rushed to the emergency room. I was laying on what could have been my deathbed.

"Here I was, thirty-three years old and for the first time in my life my parents told me they loved me. I don't believe there's a greater force on earth than the three words 'I love you,' – other than the

Divine Force. And Gopee, believe me, I know how it feels when you think no one loves you."

"No One to Turn to"

He continued, "I wanted to quit the drug business right there and then and go home with my parents, but the money and power made me stay. I got over the gunshot and put together the largest drug ring of its type in America. I became even richer, but nothing seemed to satisfy me anymore. I was alone.

"One day, I was arrested on a murder charge and was told I would die in the electric chair."

"You?" said Gopee, "I can't believe that! Man, it must have been scary. What did you do?"

"Well, I had forgotten about my Mom and Dad being Christians. They were praying-type Christians and they kept me before God for forty years. I was sent to prison . . . lost everything . . . all the money, all the power, all the so called friends."

The man looked at Gopee and explained, "You see, we always find out too late that there are no real friends in the gangs. When it comes to dying, you're living for *them*. They will always let you down." Gopee's eyes were as big as saucers.

The Voice

"All the while in prison, I was trying to get out with the help of my lawyers, but failed. Oh, the murder charge had been dropped to a manslaughter charge by now, and I was doing five years. I walked across the prison yard angry at everyone and everything. I thought, 'I've got nothing left – no hope.' But, then this Voice spoke to my heart."

Gopee looked up into the man's eyes as if to say, "Man, you're losing it!" But the story held Gopee's attention and he wanted to hear more.

He told Gopee how this Voice said, "You've had everything the world has to offer and look where it got you. Now turn your life over to Me and I will set you free."

Then, with great joy, he exclaimed, "I asked Jesus to come into my life and be my Lord and my Friend. He became my big brother."

"I wish I had a big brother," *he said with a twinge of jealousy in his voice.*

Gopee's eyes lit up. "I wish I had a big brother," he said with a twinge of jealousy in his voice.

Looking for an Escape

Bewilderment filled Gopee's face, "Man, how did you get out of the gang and all?"

But before the man could answer, a booming voice thurdered, "Gopee!" Bear was standing right there!

"Dude is going to kill me!" Gopee muttered looking for an escape path. Fear found the path as Gopee made for the street, and Bear followed right behind him.

Not knowing exactly what was taking place, the man called out, "Come back again, son!"

16

"Preach It, Brother!"

Gopee didn't stop running until he reached the house, and neither did Bear. Dude was there, but crazy from the drugs he was doing. His blood-shot eyes reddened even more when Bear told him where he found Gopee, "Right in front of the church!"

Dude raged, "I thought I told you to stay away from them church people!"

Gopee knew he was in trouble! His life would be on the line if Dude found out that the man was talking to him about Jesus, so he did the only thing he knew to do: he lied.

"Man, the guy wanted to have sex . . . and Bear messed it all up!"

"Yes, Yes!"

Dude just stared at Gopee with those wild eyes seemingly forever, then he reached out and grabbed Bear by the neck and kissed him. Dude was laughing, "See Mr. Gopee, I told you them people were crazy!"

Gopee finally breathed, and even smiled slightly, thinking that Dude was talking more about himself than anyone else. No one expected what happened next.

Dude jumped up onto the desk, mocking a street preacher. Bear got into the act by kneeling and shouting, "Yes, Yes! Preach it, Brother!" This brought the other gang members into the room, and soon everyone was encouraging Dude.

Dude jumped up onto the desk, mocking a street preacher.

"Jesus will forgive your sins! Come sinners, let Him set you free!" Laughing and shoving each other to be first, the other gang members followed Bear's example, yelling "Preach it! Yes, preach it!"

Dude must have believed Gopee's lie about the man at the church. Gopee smiled more in relief than at Dude's act. Actually, what Dude was saying concerning Jesus' forgiveness stuck deep in Gopee's heart. It was all he could think about as he tried to sleep that night.

Would they Meet Again?

Between tosses and turns, Gopee kept thinking how the man at church was so different from anyone else he had ever met. For all he had been through, this man seemed genuinely contented with life.

Happiness was something Gopee always dreamed for, but never seemed to attain. His last waking thoughts were in the hope he would see the man again, then his eyes closed.

17

Dude's "Old Man"

Delivering drugs the next day for Dude, Gopee's thoughts were constantly returning to what the man said about Jesus loving him. "And I love you, too!" played over and over in Gopee's mind.

Strangely, he thought of Dude's preaching, and wondered how he knew so much about Jesus. He might even ask Dude about it, when he wasn't strung out on drugs.

Dude was like a wild animal now. He didn't care what he did anymore. He would have sex with Bear and his friends right in front of the gang. The more drugs he took, the worse it became. Then one day, Dude was sitting on the front porch in one of the old chairs. To Gopee, Dude didn't look high, so he walked over to him, "Mind if I sit down?"

Dude was amiable, "Yeah, man. Sit down, sit down!"

Gopee lowered himself into an old recliner one of the other gang members found discarded on the sidewalk. Gopee wanted to start asking Dude so many questions that his head was spinning.

The Preacher's Kid

"What's up man?" Dude was looking right at Gopee, which made him even more uncomfortable.

Finally, Gopee just went for broke, "Dude, how do you know so much about this Jesus? It seems like you're afraid of Him."

Now he'd done it, he thought. Gopee began to steel himself for the inevitable blows as Dude would beat the devil out of him. But Dude didn't react that way. He just looked at Gopee for a long time. Then he got up and walked over in front of Gopee. Surely, Dude was getting ready to kick him.

Instead, he made his confession, "Man, I used to be a preacher's son." Gopee's face must have shown great shock because Dude laughed and continued.

"My Old Man would make me go to church every time the doors opened. I had to sit there and listen to him tell all the people about Jesus and how He loved them. I went to the Sunday School class and heard the teacher tell us 'Jesus loves me, this I know for the Bible tells me so.' My Old Man . . ."

"Hey, what's Sunday School?" Gopee wanted to know.

"Oh," Dude replied, "it's where kids go into a

class with a teacher and they talk about things."

"What kind of things?" Gopee asked.

"Oh, you know, going out on wiener roasts and things like that." Dude was searching, "And Jesus and all that stuff."

Gopee didn't know. He had never been to a Sunday School before, but he didn't want Dude to learn that. Not to seem ignorant, he said, "Oh, yeah, like that man who gave me the little booklet the other day?"

Dude overlooked the obvious connection, "Yeah, something like that. But I used to hear my Old Man stand there and preach love and peace to all them people in the church."

"It Won't Hurt"

These words brought bitter memories for Dude and the anger was building. Gopee could see it in his eyes, and *Gopee could see it in his eyes, and hear it in his voice.*

hear it in his voice, "And when we got home, my Old Man would yell and hit my mother."

Dude took a deep breath, then expelled it with, "He hit me, too, for every little thing I did!" Dude stared as some invisible screen images played out before him.

"One day, I heard my little sister crying in her room. I didn't know what was wrong. I new my Old Man hadn't whipped her. I always wondered why he never did. But that day, I found out why."

Dude began to talk through tightened lips," My Old Man was in bed with her!" He paused and then said, "I opened the door to see why she was crying. He was on top of her and trying to tell her to be quiet. 'It won't hurt,' he insisted. She was only 11 at the time. I was 13 then."

Dude's anger punctuated every word, "My Old Man was telling my sister how Jesus loved her and how *he* loved her – and this was the way Jesus wanted to let her know she was loved."

Dude kicked an empty beer car across the yard then rubbed his eyes.

Gopee could see Dude was upset, "If you don't want to talk about it, it's okay."

Dude looked down at Gopee. For a brief moment, he saw himself looking up so innocently concerned. That was a lifetime ago, he thought, as his mind drifted back.

HE PULLED THE TRIGGER!

"Just pop him when he's not looking." The gang leader pushed the revolver into Dude's young hand. He trembled at the thought of seeing someone die, but he had to do it or be alone on the streets. He looked at the pusher who was working the gang's territory, "Look, it's him or us!" The leader jabbed Dude's shoulder, "Are you in or out?"

Fear took a backseat, "I'm in!" Dude lifted the pistol, and tried to stop shaking.

"Just walk up to him, point the gun, pull the trigger and run. We'll cover for you. Okay?" Dude nodded, but the leader stopped him, "You'll be a real righteous Dude, if you do him right."

The word righteous brought a twinge of guilty anger, "Just do it!"

"Sure, brother, just do the deed!"

"Sure, brother, just do the deed!"

The scene played once again as the 14 year old walked directly toward the pusher. His back was to Dude when he pulled the pistol from under his coat, then the man turned to see the pointing barrel. Dude hadn't remembered his face again for sometime, but now he saw the same smile instantly become panic and then explode with the gun blast.

"Run, you mother, run," the leader was screaming in Dude's ear and pushing him. Then Dude began to run, and run, and run. When he found a dark place in an abandoned building he stopped and waited for the police to take him away. They never came.

"You Nosy Little Snot!"

He spent the night awake, then carefully walked back to the gang's hideout. Once there, he was welcomed as a hero. His days as a gang member had started.

"I was only 14." Dude said out loud, "I didn't know what I wanted out of life. I just knew I didn't want to be home anymore. When I shot the guy, the gang thought I was hot stuff. I wasn't even sure if I killed him.

"Did you ever kill anyone else, Dude?"

They were all laughing and giving me the high sign." Dude never admitted that he was really sick to his stomach; he just said, "After awhile, it even felt good!"

"Did you ever kill anyone else, Dude?" Gopee said admiring his accomplishment.

"Did I kill anyone else?" Dude repeated, "Yeah, I went back and killed that stinkin' Old Man of mine. I sent his dirty, rotten tail to hell where he belonged?"

Dude got right up in Gopee's face, "That's why I don't believe in Jesus and that's why I don't want you or any of the others talking to anyone about it."

Then Dude shouted, "You hear me?"

Gopee literally jumped back.

"Now get your little fanny up and out of here you nosey little snot!" Dude backed away and stomped off into the house.

Gopee gulped air for a moment, then quickly returned to delivering drugs.

18

"What's a Christian?"

Back on the street, away from Dude's anger, Gopee repeatedly thought of the man at the church. His gentle kindness was so opposite to Dude, yet he was once a gang leader, too. And if this man got out, then Gopee wanted to know how to do it without getting killed. Why did he leave all that money? The questions kept coming until Gopee knew he just had to meet him again.

Friday night, at 10th and Vine, Gopee made one of his last drops. It was a place where the rich kids hung out. He was on his way back to the house, when someone called, "Hey! How you doing?"

There he was, that man – handing tracts on the corner again. Gopee thought he better ignore him, and walked by looking down at the concrete.

"Hey, man," the man repeated, coming after Gopee, "I want to talk to you some more."

"Well, I don't want to talk to you!" Gopee lied,

continuing to walk.

"Dude told me about your kind and that his Old Man was a preacher and how this Jesus wanted his little sister to show him how she loved him too." Gopee stopped for emphasis, "Dude's Old Man raped his sister and beat his mother, so he killed his Old Man for it."

Gopee watched as tears began to roll down his face and onto the street.

Saved from What?

The man sat Gopee down on the curb and took a seat next to him. Gopee watched as tears began to roll down his face and onto the street. He looked at Gopee with a look he had never seen before – it was one of compassion and love for this street kid. The countenance on his face was more compelling than anything he could say or do.

"Son, that wasn't Jesus. He doesn't hurt people. He gave His life so we can be set free from drugs, and sin, and all those things the devil does – and causes us to do. That preacher was not truly a Christian."

"What's a Christian?" Gopee stopped him.

The man smiled, "A Christian is someone who has given his or her life to Jesus Christ. Jesus forgives them of all their sins if they turn from the kind of life they used to have and start living for Him, doing what He tells them to do. Just like He did for me when I became a Christian, and was saved."

"What was you saved from?" Gopee asked.

It was a good question, and the man realized it could only be answered over a meal, "Hey, let's get a Coke and a sandwich and I'll tell you!"

Food always sounded good to Gopee, "Okay!"

19

"Yeah, Maybe Later"

Across the street, they entered a small sandwich shop, sat down and ordered Cokes. Gopee asked if he could have some lemon pie.

"I never had a piece of lemon pie in my whole life!"

"You can have a whole pie, if you want to," the man laughed.

Soon their sandwiches arrived, and in between bites and swallows, the man retold his story of the gangs he had belonged to and led. Gopee was entranced. He told the young man how he literally made fortunes – and about the boats, big houses, the girls, and the places he traveled. Then he related how his enemies, and even his lieutenants, tried to kill him.

"I was even arrested on a first degree murder charge," he said. Again, Gopee's mouth opened almost as wide as his eyes.

"You? You were really arrested for murder?" he

blurted out, forgetting they were in a restaurant, then he whispered, "You? For murder!"

Gopee wanted more details, but you don't ask someone who they killed. Yet this man didn't look like a killer to Gopee. No, this guy was somebody who really cared about you.

Somebody Prayed!

"I was in prison facing the death penalty for two years," the man shook his head, "They even tried to get me killed behind bars."

The man sat up, nibbled on the sandwich, then asked, "Do you know why I didn't die in prison, son?" Gopee shook his head.

"Because my mother and father were praying Christians, and every day they were asking God to protect me and not let me die in that place. That's why!"

Gopee was amazed. He had to know more about how God got this man out of prison. It was almost frustrating for Gopee to watch him eat. Gopee just wanted him to finish his story.

Finally he swallowed and began again, "I thought I had a lot of friends in my gang. We had gone together from being penny-ante street thugs to organized crime. I was the king-pin in our drug business, but when I went to prison, suddenly I didn't have any friends anymore. They vanished when the money did. When you're in prison, no one wants to know you."

"But how did you get out?" Gopee wasn't eating. "You must have really known somebody – right?"

The man smiled and motioned for Gopee to eat, "Son, I didn't have any connections. I didn't know anybody anymore. But I knew my parents were praying for me." He took another bite of

"I never had anybody pray for me. Why would you?"

his sandwich creating just the right dramatic pause, "And I have been praying for you!"

Gopee dropped his head, "I never had anybody pray for me. Why would *you?*"

The man smiled, took another bite, and quietly said, "Because I see me in you."

Still Hurt

Gopee couldn't grasp that thought. All he wanted to know was: "Yeah, but how did you get out of prison?"

"I had some lawyers who tried everything in their power to get me out, yet after all they did, I was still there."

"So what did you do?" Gopee persisted. "Did you

break out or escape?"

"No," the man laughed, "You see, I had no place to go and no one to turn to for help . . . at least, that's what I thought." He bit into his sandwich.

Gopee imagined that maybe he bribed someone, or that surely he knew a high official who helped him out.

"Just when I thought I had nothing left, and no one to turn to, Jesus came into my life. I read about Him in a little Gideon New Testament Bible. It told me how much Jesus loves me . . . that He died in my place."

The man shifted his weight in his seat, "You see I should have died for all the sins and wicked things I had done, but Jesus forgave me and set me free from all the shame and guilt."

This sounded good to Gopee, but now *his* shame surfaced. "But nobody cares what happens to people like me." Gopee was still hurt, "I was at that church and heard what those people said. They don't want freaks like me in their church."

"Jesus wants you in His church, and I want you in my church." The man leaned over, "How about coming with me this Sunday, will you?"

"No . . . I can't." Gopee shook his head.

The Door Closed

Wise in the ways of the streets, the man knew

enough not to press the issue, "Okay, maybe later."

Gopee said in relief, "Yeah, maybe later."

They finished their food. "That's the best pie, I have ever eaten," Gopee said licking the spoon. For the first time he noticed the restaurant's wall clock. "Man, I've got to get. I'm late and Dude'll kill me!" Gopee was moving toward the door.

"Hey, if you ever need any help, I'll be around here or some of the guys that I work with will be, okay?"

Gopee probably said, "Okay," but the door closed so quickly behind him, no one heard. All the man could do was to turn back to where Gopee had been seated – and pray.

20

A Frightening Scene

Fortunately for Gopee, Dude was already passed out on beer and drugs. If he hurried he could make his next drop and no one would ever know he had been late. No one ever did.

Slowly, two weeks passed by. This day Dude got high on crack. To entertain himself, he started spinning his pistol like a cowboy, and trying to quick draw it from his pants pocket.

"Put that away, man, you're gonna kill somebody!" Bear's booming voice stopped Dude.

Instead of obeying, Dude came over to Bear and put the gun to his head saying, "You think you're boss now? I'll blow your damn head off you mother . . ."

The cocking of another gun behind Dude's ear silenced him in mid-sentence. It was one of Bear's friends.

"Move and I'll blow your head off!" he said.

Dude lowered his gun, and protested, "Hell, I was only joking."

Bear took the revolver from Dude's hand, and stared. Gopee had watched the whole thing and was glad it was coming to an end, so he thought. Then, he noticed it wasn't over with Bear.

"You stupid %@#! You've let drugs fry your crazy brains" Bear bellowed. "And nobody puts a gun to my head and lives to tell about it!"

The barrel of the 357 Magnum filled Dude's mouth.

By now there were more of Bear's friends surrounding Dude, and they jumped him, grabbing his hair and pulling his head back. The barrel of the 357 Magnum filled Dude's mouth. He tried to say, "You can't kill me, I'm the boss," but the gun barrel garbled his words.

Next, the back of Dude's head exploded onto the wall. Bear had pulled the trigger. Dude's limp body crumpled to the floor. Bear was standing over him with the gun barrel still giving off a wisp of smoke.

A Suicide?

Gopee was paralyzed with fear. He had never seen anyone shot that way before, and he didn't know what Bear would do next.

The explosion caused the other gang members to come running. Bear looked at Gopee and said, "It was a suicide . . . wasn't it?" Gopee said nothing. Then Bear pointed the gun, "Wasn't it?"

Gopee nodded.

"I'm boss now," Bear barked, "Clean this mess up!"

Bear's friends put Dude's body in the trunk of a car, and that was the end of Dude. Bear became the gang's new leader, and turned even meaner than Dude – if that was possible. He made the younger kids in the gang perform all kinds of sexual acts with him and his friends, making the others watch. Gang life was becoming unbearable, and Gopee wanted out more than ever.

Just like the man in the sandwich shop who was freed from prison, Gopee was bound and determined to somehow pull himself loose from the gang.

21

Into the Night

Gopee slipped out one day, and purposely went looking for the man. He checked the church, and then the sandwich shop, yet he was nowhere to be found. But others were handing out the same tracts.

"Hey, Mister," Gopee was desperate, "can you help me?" Gopee described the man who had given him the booklet, and asked if he knew him. He did, "But he's out of town for a week!"

"Well, can you help me?"

"Sure, I'll help you," he smiled.

"These people are the smilingest people I have ever seen," Gopee thought to himself. He told the stranger his story, and ended it, "So can you help me?"

The tall man nodded, and asked, "Gopee, have you ever asked Jesus into your heart?"

"No," he replied.

"Well, that's where it begins for all of us.

Without Jesus in our heart we can never be really free from anything." He looked at the young man and asked, "Gopee, do you want Jesus to set you free?"

He thought for a second, and said, "Yes!"

Together, they prayed that night for Jesus to save Gopee from his sins, and to help him. "You need to start going to church, too," the man told him.

This was a problem for Gopee, "Those other church people don't want someone like me in their church."

"No problem, come to my church." The tall man got up, "It's just a little further down the street, and we don't mind you coming just like you are!"

"Okay," Gopee smiled, and watched the man wave and leave.

Hiding Out

It was dark and cool, but Gopee thought he should hide out until Sunday rather than go back to the house. When Sunday arrived, he made his way to the small church.

Turning the corner, he saw the flash of colored jackets ahead, and instantly backed up. It was Bear and the gang.

Gopee ran and jumped behind some shrubbery just when the group rounded the comer. He didn't even draw a breath, waiting for them to pass.

"When I get my hands on that Gopee . . ." Bear was furious, "I'm gonna make him wish he was dead." The others laughed and joined in with the threats Bear was making.

Gopee knew Bear never liked him that much anyway, and now with his wanting to go to church, he really believed Bear meant what he said. So Gopee hid until they passed, and then crossed through yards hiding out most of the day.

It wasn't until nightfall that Gopee went to the church. As he approached the building, he saw a few kids that hung around with some of the gang members. Fearing they would tell, he turned and ran down a side street.

Leaving his own turf meant he could be in a lot of trouble, but just once, he wanted to see

"When I get my hands on that Gopee...I'm going to make him wish he was dead."

what church was like. He had asked Jesus into his heart and knew this was what he was supposed to do.

The Door Creaked

Thinking all churches were the same and that Christians were like the men he had met on the streets, he found another church down the street and decided to go in. He remembered the earlier encounter where the people turned up their noses at him. Gopee convinced himself, "Surely, these people will be different."

The service had already started. He opened the door and tried to step in quietly, but the door squeaked. Everyone turned to see who was coming in late, and when they saw it was Gopee, surprise filled their faces. Everyone had on new clothes it seemed to Gopee, while his clothes were well worn.

The clean, scrubbed faces stared in disbelief as this unwashed, oily haired boy with the torn shoes sat down in the last row. Gopee didn't want to make a scene, he just longed to hear more about Jesus, his new-found Savior.

No one really bothered to meet Gopee that night. They sang songs he had never heard before, but no one offered him a hymnal. The minister stood up and talked, although he didn't say much about Jesus – at least not like the men with the tracts did.

Finally, the service was over, and while the final prayer was being said, Gopee slipped out the door. The door creaked again, but no one came after him. Nobody asked him if he needed help, or to invite him back. Gopee disappeared into the night.

No More Loneliness

Gopee walked alone, humming one of the songs he had heard, and thinking aloud. It was almost like he was talking to God. He thought, "Well, so what no one talked to me; I liked those songs. I think I'll go back next Sunday."

He smiled, and then a large hand grabbed him and then another. Bear and the gang surrounded him.

Much later, Gopee's body was found – abused, tortured, and mutilated. For Gopee, his endless days of loneliness were now over. No one would ever have the chance to accept or reject, or love him in spite of his ragged clothes and dirty face. People wouldn't mutter about his appearance anymore, or worry if he was going to sit by them.

Gopee was in heaven, listening to more songs he had never heard, washed and clean before his Lord Jesus Christ. And after all the singing and praising, when they sit down to supper, perhaps there will be a slice of lemon pie for Gopee. What do you think?

When you get to heaven, you can see for yourself!

Epilogue

Gopee's real name was Robert, I am the "man with the tract" and your church is where people like Gopee pass by everyday.

As I look at the world around me, I wonder, "Just how many others are like Gopee, searching for a way out of their life in gangs, streets and sin. I also wonder how many of us tend to cross to the other side of the street when we see a life worn, battered, and bruised.

How many times have we, who are born again Christians, "left someone for dead" in this world when we should have helped to clean and bandage their wounds? Only God knows.

Perhaps this true story will cause you to see the "invisible people" around you, those who move through our lives with whom we never talk or share our faith.

If you are like me, you remember the times when only a small amount of evangelism incurred a great deal of wrath from some unfortunate soul – or you were branded "preacher" or "fanatic."

I pray this story has stirred something deep within you – especially since there are so many lost souls who lay awake at night questioning if God can really help them.

If you have accepted Christ you know He can, because Jesus has lifted you from your life of sin and is with you even today.

The streets are truly wheat fields ready to be harvested, and we desperately need more committed workers.

Be ready. It may be sooner than you think when someone asks, "Hey, Mister, can you help me?"

FOOD FOR THOUGHT

Countless teens on the street need our assistance. They truly need to know Jesus loves them. Here are just a few of the problems we must work and pray to change:*

- There are over 500,000 runaway and "throwaway" teens on the streets of the U.S.
- Over 1 million teens have a drug dependency.
- There are more than 730,000 members of 21,000 gangs in 2,300 U.S. cities.
- Every 13 seconds a teenager contracts a sexual transmitted disease.
- We have lost more teens to suicide in the last decade than we lost in the entire Vietnam War.

*Sources: U.S. Dept. Of Justice; Partnership for a Drug-Free America; National Youth Gang Center; New York Times, National Household Survey on Drug Abuse.

To schedule the author for speaking engagements, or for more information on how you or your church can help, please contact:

BILL SAYE
MINISTRIES
1320 S. MADISON AVENUE
DOUGLAS, GA 31533

PHONE: 912-389-0581
INTERNET: www.billsaye.org
EMAIL: billsaye@alltel.net

You are encouraged to become a partner in this vital outreach. Your gift of any size to Bill Saye Ministries will touch and impact many lives.

Thanks for your prayer and support – and be ready to respond when someone asks, "Hey, Mister, can you help me?"